Passive Income

A Complete Step-by-Step Guide to Building Multiple Streams of Income and Finally Gain Freedom and Financial Independence

By Timothy Turner

Table of Contents

Prologue

"Making money while you sleep."

It sounds good, doesn't it? This is the desire of many people and some have succeeded in earning passive income from several streams. If your goal is to earn money while you sleep, you have to reach a certain point where every asset you own will earn money for you. However, to reach this point is not as easy as it sounds. You will need to dedicate money, time, and work. Passive income is defined as the process where money is earned with little activity when compared to a full time job through a number of ventures that demand little upkeep or daily effort on the person's part.

You will be able to earn passive income whether you are someone who has extra money you want to invest or an entrepreneur with an amazing business plan. On the most basic level, you will be able to earn money through passive income opportunities with considerably less effort, but you should bear in mind that the term can be a bit deceptive because this type of income is not completely passive. Becoming an expert of generating passive income does not mean that you will do nothing and only watch the cash rolling in. If your goal is money with no effort, you will most probably get scammed or take a very dangerous risk of facing a bad situation.

Passive income can result in you having more free time, but in order for you to get to this point you will have to work, sometimes hard because it may take a lot of hustle depending on the different passive income ideas you will want to follow. This amount of work will become less or at least remain the same once the business is ready while your gains will continue to increase.

One other thing you should keep in mind is that passive income will take time to develop. You may think about pursuing this type of hustle, as many do, but you are not taking any action like most people. Most of those people will be stuck on the analysis stage and never actually take that extremely important step to their financial freedom. Your first days, after you decide to take this step and earn passive income, will be dedicated to educating yourself on finance, business, and investments.

Do not try to learn everything there is out there because they will never be enough and will only confuse you. In other words, do not be afraid to fail. You will see that those extremely successful people will tell you that their failures are what allowed them to be where they are today. Anybody can do it. Anybody can start earning passive income and reach a point where he or she has achieved financial freedom. Let us see how through this complete guide of how to earn passive income.

In the first chapter, we will present you with the different streams of income and mainly the ones successful people use to better understand later the gist of passive income. In the second chapter, we will introduce you to robo advisors which are a great way for you to invest your money without the hustle of having to build and manage your investment portfolio. Let the robo advisors do those things for you.

In the third chapter, we will present you the different ways you can build your wealth through passive real estate investing. Passive real estate investing is a great way to multiply your money without having to deal with the various problems and stress an active investor has to go through with investment properties. In the fourth chapter, we will show you another great stream of passive income that is opening and maintaining a high-yield savings account. This stream of passive income is often characterized as the simplest, safest, and most boring investment that was ever created and this may have some truth in it. Let us see in the fourth chapter why.

In the fifth chapter, we will present you with the various things you need to know in order to invest in certificates of deposit. This stream of passive income has many benefits, but if you need immediate access to your money, this is not the best choice for you. They usually have a time frame during which you will not be able to touch them. However, they also perfect for accumulating your money if you can get passed through this little drawback. More about this passive income option, in chapter five.

In the sixth chapter, we will show you all the things you need to consider and plan when you decide to earn a considerable amount of passive income through Airbnb©. This is a great option that you can later turn into a full business by dedicating more of your time to plan things though. Let's find more about this great passive income option in chapter six. In the seventh chapter, we will show you the last effective way for you to be able to earn the passive income that could set you on the right track of gaining your financial freedom. This las source of passive income is Index Funds. Let us learn more about them in the seventh and final chapter.

The Different Streams of Income

Usually, people are making money from one source of income or two. However, did you know that there are different streams of income you can start making money off? Streams of income that even millionaires apply? There are more on how to earn money that you probably know of. The internet is filled with books and articles on how to get rich quickly and be a millionaire overnight, but most people are not aware of the different ways they will be able to earn more money and live comfortably or are simply too afraid of the risks involved and do nothing about it. It may be also the fact that some people do not want to make millions of dollars in a few years, but they wish to reduce the time they spend each day on making money from their main source of income, which is their full-time job.

Typically, there are three ways to be able to earn money:

Capital gains:

Usually, when we refer to capital gains we talk about an underlying asset that has risen in value and then sold for profit. A capital asset is almost every personal item you own such as investments, a car, or real estate. However, if you own a business, the assets of your business are not capital assets including supplies for business purposes, equipment, and inventory. Also, capital assets are not any songs you have produced or the copyrights to your creations. There is a simple investing concept that has to do with selling high and buying low.

If you have sold anything including a car, a house, stocks, gold coins, you most probably have a capital loss or gain. When compared to a standard salary, capital gains are taxed with a more favorable rate and this is the reason why this income stream is considered to have a greater effect on your pocket. However, not all capital gains are the same and there are some exceptions to the above fact. The tax rate of a capital gain is based on the two categories of capital gain, which are the following:

- ✓ Short-term capital gain
- ✓ Long-term capital gain

When we refer to short-term capital gains, we include profits that come from the sale of an asset you had ownership for approximately a year or less. This capital gain does not have the benefits of a special tax rate since it is taxed as your salary does. The exact opposite is long-term capital gain. If you own this asset form more than a year, you will benefit from a less tax rate on your gains. These two categories were created to enhance long-term investments in the economy.

Labour:

The most common and essential way of making money is labor, a process where your time is exchanged for money. Earned income, which is one of the various streams of income is considered to be the money you earn through spending your time on it, for instance through working for someone. This is the part where your quality of life will be endangered to suffer the most since you will trade valuable time for money. Most jobs will pay enough for you to not be broke.

The most common reason why people are not able to move on from making money through their job is that it offers them a comfort zone. Unfortunately, this comfort zone is a double-edged knife and can become your biggest enemy since it will keep you from having an amazing life. In other words, you will spend most of your life earning money only from this income stream and you will not have enough money to be wealthy and have a comfortable life. To quote the words from the Rat Race to Financial Freedom:

"Comfort is your biggest trap and coming out of comfort zone your biggest enemy"

Passive income:

Your asset will generate income, but its value is not altered when the revenues are generated. You will know how much you make from passive income from the difference between the income and the expenses needed when you manage the asset.

Profit Income:

Through profit income, you earn money from selling a product for more than it costed you to make. For example, shirts, laptops, mobile phones, no matter if you are at the retail or on a wholesale level. To earn profits you have to be an entrepreneur. To start a business, you will probably need a huge investment or begin with a small business for profit with a small investment. However, you should keep in mind that this will require a lot of your time, especially through your first steps, until you are able to manage your business very well and let make money on its own.

Being an entrepreneur demands a different type of mindset as well as the capability of taking risks. Most people in a job are used to the stream of earning income and wish to make the move towards this category at a certain stage of their careers. However, they find it very difficult to make this move, because they are afraid of the added risks. This fear is often justified due to the constraints many people have on their needs and due to family reasons.

We will analyze in later chapters what an entrepreneur is, but generally, you will have to make a product or sell a service and manage both your clients and sells very well. Most people think that the only viable tools through which they can earn money are the streams of Earned Income and Profit Income. However, they don't know or forget that there are more serious and reliable ways to generate your wealth.

Interest Income:

When you lend your money to someone else, for example, placing them in a bank or lending them to the government by buying Treasury Bills, you earn money from the stream of Interest Income. This is also one of the top choices of passive income, where no active involvement is necessary once you make the investment. Many people do not understand the amount of wealth they will be able to generate with the Interest Income stream, but when it is linked with compound interest and the fact that it is a passive income with practically no serious risks, it can be better than the two sources of income we mentioned before.

Compound interest is the interest that is added to the initial sum of money, which includes the accumulated interest of all the previous periods of a loan or a deposit. According to Warren Buffet:

"My wealth has come from a combination of living in America, some lucky genes, and compound interest."

Let us take a closer look at how compound interest works. Let's say that you have a mortgage of $20.000 to be paid in 30 years and your interest is 5%. The principal and interest payment will be $1.073,64 and for this amount of money, you will be making 360 payments. On your first payment of this amount, only $240,31 will go to pay the principal amount and $833,33 will go to the interest. As months pass, a few more money will go for the payment of the principal amount of money to slowly bring down the amount. If you calculate all the payments, which are 360 x $1.073,64, the money you will pay will be a total of $386.510,40 when the 30 year period is over. In other words, the interest you paid was $186.510,40.

If you could take $200.000 and simply divided this amount to 360 payments, you would have to pay each month $555,55. From this example, you see how interest can cause us harm when it works against us. Let us see an example where interest is working for you by using the same amount of $200.000, the same payment scheme with 360 monthly payments with 5% interest, and the same period of 30 years.

If for 30 years you were able to put $1.073,64 each month in an interest-bearing account and earn a 5% interest, at the end of the 30 years you would have $902.066. If the interest was higher at 8%, in thirty years you will have $1.622.517. Albert Einstein knew that compound interest can change lives. In his words:

"Compound interest is the eighth wonder of the world. He who understands it, earns it. He who doesn't, pays it."

17

Dividend Income:

This stream of income has the potential to be better than Interest Income. It is also considered to be a passive income and it will make you a shareholder of a company. Through this income stream, you will be able to earn money as a return of the company shares you will own. The dividend is announced by most companies when the year ends. Even though it sounds very good, this is one of the most neglected source of income. If you are able to make a good investment on the ex-dividend dates of companies, the returns from Dividend Income will surpass the ones of Interest Income due to the fact that you will also be a member of the Capital Gains the share price will go through.

To better understand the concept of dividend income, it refers to the distribution of the earnings a company has to its shareholders from mutual funds or stocks that you own. All companies are able to choose several things to do with the earnings they generate. For instance, they are able to keep their earning within their business in order to broaden their operations, accumulate wealth, or pay off their debts. They can also buy shares with their profits or distribute a part of their profits to their shareholders in stock or cash, something that is defined as dividend. Most companies that choose this payment method do so quarterly, however, monthly or annual dividends are not unusual.

If you decide to pursue this stream of income, you will come across the term "qualified dividend". In order for you to be qualified for a low tax rate, the dividend you receive must:

✓ Have been paid by a qualified foreign corporation or have been paid by a United States corporation.

✓ Have the stock for more than 60 days during a period of 121 days starting 60 days prior to the ex-dividend date. A preferred stock requires to hold it for 90 days out of a period of 181 days, starting 90 days prior to the ex-dividend date of the stock.

Some examples of dividends that are not deemed as "qualified dividends" are money given from when a company sells its property or else capital gain distributions, dividends paid on credit union and bank deposits, dividends from an organization that is exempt from tax, and particular pass-through dividends.

Rental Income:

Another stream of income is the rental income which is money you receive as a result of your renting an asset that you own such as a building or a house. This stream of income is also considered better than the other 4 types we mentioned before, however, it has some drawbacks when compared to the other streams we analyzed.

For instance, this type of investment requires a larger amount of money to make such an asset that will offer you a regular, monthly, rental income. Since the amount of money you will have to invest is huge, you may not be able to creat many assets throughout your life, unless you have other ways to generate income.

When you compare it to the other streams of income, it will be easy to earn Dividend Income or Interest Income with an investment of the amount INR 1.000; however, you will not be able to earn Rental Income with such small amount of cash invested. Another important drawback of this stream is the illiquidity of your assets. If you decide to rearrange your portfolio, it may be difficult for you to liquefy you assets quickly and will need a lot of planning to do so.

Royalty Income:

Through this stream of income, you will earn money resulting from allowing someone to use your ideas, processes, or products. The ones who use your product will do all the hard work and the revenues with you getting a small percentage of whatever money they earn. For example, if you have a shop under the name of a franchise, you will pay royalties to the franchise for using their marketing, their processes, their logo, etc. This is royalty income for their part. If you are an author, you will be paid for every book you sell.

This stream of income has its challenges too. The biggest one is creating something that is unique and then, be able to repeat it. Special skills may be required for the asset you create, but once it is out there, you will have no limit to the amount of money you will earn.

Those were the most common sources of income that are used by millionaires. The truth of the matter is that not all millionaires use all of these streams. In fact, Warren Buffet, who is a billionaire, uses Capital Gains and Dividend Income. However, he did not earn Capital Gains on everything there is, he specialized in Capital Gains of stock market companies. He developed his skills that had to do with valuing and investing in companies. This way he was able to be a millionaire and then turn into a billionaire.

Another example of famous people that managed to accumulate wealth through multiple streams of income is Bill Gates. He was able to generate his income through Royalty Income and Profit Income streams. Bill Gates founded a company and came up with an asset that we know today as "Windows". Then, he used this asset to completely change the way we work with computers.

The bottom line is that you should focus on how you will be able to make money from these income streams. Then, you can be the best, by developing your skills, in a small part of the particular income streams you created. You should also keep in mind that if you search for people that became millionaires through the Earned income stream, you will find very few. This happens because this is the stream where out time is used least efficiently, and there are limits to the hours we are able to spend there each day.

There is also the limit of the amount of money we will be able to earn from this type of stream. All the other streams of income we analyzed are not entirely dependent on the time we place in them and thus we are able to dedicate as many hours as we wish to become better, accumulate wealth, and achieve financial freedom. Let us move on to the various ways we will be able to turn this into reality.

Robo- Investing

If you are a full-time investor or you are just making your first steps in investing, robo advisors will offer you the chance to automate investing if you wish. Robo advisors will build a fully diversified portfolio based on the preferences of investors, for this reason, they are called automated investment services.

Essentially, they are investment tools that use computer software and algorithms to manage and create an investor's portfolio. This is achieved through a questionnaire given to an investor to conclude your risk tolerance, investment preferences, and investment goals. Then, the robo advisor will offer you the right portfolio, based on your answers, to buy. When this step is complete, the robo advisor will automatically build a diversified investment portfolio as well as choose the funds on your behalf.

This way of managing your investments is a relatively low-cost method that places your portfolio on autopilot. Generally, investors are able to manage and build their portfolio with the following ways:

- ✓ They hire a financial advisor to make a curated portfolio
- ✓ They pick investments themselves
- ✓ They use a robo advisor to make their portfolio

With robo advisors, you will replace the job of a financial advisor and gain the time you will spend by choosing to build a portfolio yourself. This way you will be able to dedicate the time you freed into creating other sources of passive income. You will have to open a robo manager account and then answer the questions you will be given through the online questionnaire. Once you invest your funds, your portfolio will be rearranged to meet the target allocation. Some of the robo advisors offer particular securities when it comes to tax-loss harvesting which will help you lessen the amount of money you will have to pay on taxes.

The different types of investors that can benefit from using robo advisors are the following:

✓ Beginner Investors: Such investors do not yet have the necessary financial knowledge to proceed in well-informed investment decisions and are comfortable with letting the management of their portfolio to online services with less human assistance or no human assistance at all.

✓ Professional Investors: Such investors may wish to place their portfolio on automatic pilot since they may not have the time to manage it themselves because they are chasing after other sources of passive income or their portfolio is too big to manage.

✓ Investors that Follow Simple Strategies: A simple strategy for the allocation of your assets may be 60% for stocks and 40% for bonds. These strategies do not require the assistance of a financial advisor who will continuously rebalance your account.

✓ Investors with a Do-It-Yourself Approach: If you don't want to hire a financial advisor and wish to have more free time from having to choose the investments you make on your own, you will be able to get help from a robo advisor to select your investments for you, place trades on your account, and rebalance them.

However, the solution of automated management of your investment portfolio is not ideal for the following types of investors:

- ✓ Investors who want Human Assistance: Even though there are some robo advisors who will offer you human assistance with the additional costs, you will interact with them through the internet. If you seek someone who you will be able to meet with, in person and stay with you for a long time, robo advisor is not the one to choose.
- ✓ Investors who Have Many Investment Accounts: If you are an investor that has to manage benefit packages of your company as well as manage many different accounts, this automation process of robo advisor is not suitable for your needs.
- ✓ Investors that Require a Tailored Management: You will not be able to get customized advice or plans on how much money you will have to save or whether you should use a Traditional IRA or a Roth IRA.

By using an algorithm for your investments, you will get passive income from investing from the comfort of your home, and essentially you will have the time to create other streams of income while you let a computer take care of this part of your passive income plan. There are other benefits of using a robo advisor aside from the automated process that makes investing fall into the category of passive income.

For instance, you will avoid making crucial mistakes. It is a fact that there have been many cases of investors that fail or get very poor outcomes from their investments due to mistakes that have to do with their behavior and mindset. Investors are humans and as humans, we tend to make emotional decisions based on our instincts. Robo advisor software will not make those mistakes.

Also, through the automated process, the software of the robo advisor will take care of all the investment process. You will not have to worry about altering your portfolio or invest less or more money based on the market factor. You will not even be required to enter your account to place trades. Another thing to consider is that you will be able to make smaller investments at a lower cost. Financial advisor firms will typically ask for a higher amount of money from the investor to invest at the beginning and incur fees that can be higher when compared to those that robo advisors charge. You will also not have to worry if the investing recommendation the broker makes is appropriate for you.

When it comes to the fees the robo advisor will charge you, typically, you will have to pay a service fee that can be settled through a percentage of the assets or through a fixed monthly fee that varies from $15 to $200 per month and it depends on the value of your portfolio. If the payment is done through percentages of the assets you may see fees of approximately 0.15% to 0.50% based on the value of your account for each year. For example, if your account is worth $100.000, a 0.15% fee will be translated to $500 per year.

You will also have to pay for any expenses that are linked with investments that are used by the robo advisors. For instance, exchange-traded funds, as well as mutual funds, will have expense ratios. Those fees will be deducted from the assets of your fund before robo advisors distribute the earnings to investors. If you are not sure that this is the method you wish to choose, some robo advisors offer a free trial period for you to check how they work before they start charging you.

You should keep in mind that most of the robo advisors you will find are using exchange-traded funds or mutual funds and not individual stocks to create your portfolio. They usually follow a passive investment method that is based on modern portfolio theory research. This method stresses the importance of the process of allocating to bonds or stocks.

Robo advisors will help you make a passive investment income through tools that will assist you in managing and building a diversified portfolio as well as show you how your accounts grow over the course of time. If you want to pay lower fees than the ones you would pay with financial advisors and have account minimus, this option is appropriate for you.

However, if you want to be a professional investor, robo advisors are not financial planners. They will not be able to offer you solutions tailored to your needs and direct you to particular investing strategies. Also, if you are close to your retirement, the allocation models of robo advisors may not assist you in the alignment of your investments with the phase of withdrawal. For this reason, they are recommended for investors who just start their careers and then, in later stages of their lives, seek a professional retirement income planner.

Passive Real Estate Investing

Real estate investing has been deemed as one of the greatest ways to create and accumulate wealth. As a matter of fact, real estate is one of the things most millionaires have in common since it is the primary way they became millionaires. In real estate investing there are active ways of investing such as managing an owning rental properties or renovating and flipping houses and there are passive ways to earn money that do not require from the investors to take on an active role.

When it comes to investing, passive refers to the fact that you will not play an active role in the business you will invest in. It does not mean that you will not have to do anything since it is not as simple as deciding to invest somewhere, invest your money, and never think of it again. For example, when you purchase shares of a company, you ill not have an active role in the daily operations of the company. You will only be able to financially benefit if the company succeeds. Another example of a passive investment is investing in your friend's company that you will not help him or her run.

Even though you will make passive investments, you are still required to research and learn both before and after you place your money in. When it comes to real estate investing, there are three basic ways to passively invest:

- ✓ Through real estate crowdfunding
- ✓ Through the stock market
- ✓ Forging a partnership with an active investor and own properties

A relatively new method in real estate investing is crowdfunding, which uses crowdfunding for raising capital targeted at real estate investments. By using this method of real estate investing, every investor will be able to invest in a wide range of properties without dealing with contractors, mortgage brokers, or real estate agents. All these will be the responsibilities of the crowdfunding platform which will take care of daily tasks to make sure the completion of the investment is successful and allow the investor to receive the returns with no need to go through the process of renovating and flipping homes on his or her own.

To better understand what crowdfunding is, think of it as a way for business owners to raise money without having to ask for just one investor to make a large investment, but through reaching out to a lot of investors who are willing to contribute a small amount of money. The way to reach out, multiple investors at one is done through an online platform.

There are crowdfunding websites and many business owners choose social media platforms for this job too such as Twitter and Facebook to advertise their project to a wider audience of investors who may be interested. If you invest in passive real estate keep in mind that it is a reliable method to generate money and there have been many cases of crowdfunded real estate investments that generated annual returns of approximately 15% and more for its investors.

If you are a beginner in real estate investing or an experienced investor, you need to understand or already know that securing the necessary funds to seal a deal can pose a real challenge to your plans. Due to this fact of the real estate market, many investors take advantage of the crowdfunding method as an alternative to secure funds for their deals. Several benefits of this method are the following:

- ✓ It will increase the options an investor has for funding his or her projects while growing his or her network of other investors.
- ✓ The investor with the deal and the one who will invest in it will indulge in direct marketing through this method which can also be used as a tool for the promotion of real estate businesses.
- ✓ With the completion of successful projects, the investor will gain a good reputation and the loyalty of his or her clients.
- ✓ From the online community, the real estate business will create; it will gain access to important feedback to address any potential flaws.

If you are on the other side of the spectrum, as a passive investor who helps in the funding of a real estate business project, aside from the immense returns you will get if the project is successful, you will be able to meet other investors whose ideas you would like to fund too and thus gain more passive income. Let us see the main two options of crowdfunding that will help you build your wealth passively.

The first option is equity investments and this is the most common method of crowdfunding investors choose due to the fact that it offers a higher return than the other option which is debt investing. However, the equity investment option is not without risks. This will give the investor an equity stake in a commercial or residential property, thus making him or her a shareholder.

The return of this investment will be calculated on the property's rental income minus the costs required for the crowdsourcing platform. If the property you invested in through this method is sold, you will get your share based on its appreciation value. Usually, the payments are done every quarter. Let us see the benefits of equity investments:

✓ There are no limits on returns: On a yearly basis, you may see returns at times up to 18 to 25 percent and possibly even more since this type of investment doesn't have a cap on them.

✓ Low fees: You will have the choice to pay one annual fee to keep your shares on the property you invested in, instead of fees paid from the start or monthly fees.

✓ Tax benefits: Due to the fact that you will own a share of the investment property, you will be able to remove expenses on it from your annual income tax such as repairs or depreciation.

Some of the cons of equity investments include the fact that it is considered to be an investment with more risks since you will only be on the background when it comes to payments. In other words, if the investment property does not generate any profits, you will not get any returns on the money you invested. Also, if you wish to include more liquidity in your portfolio, then this method is not for you since it has a holding period of five to ten years.

The second method of crowdfunding investing is debt investments which mean that you as the investor will be the lender to the business that wants to carry out the project. You will receive a fixed return calculated by the interest rate of the mortgage loan the owner has and the amount of money you have put in. The payments in this method are completed every month or every quarter. Since you have indulged in debt investing when the payments are due you will be a top priority. Let us see some more benefits of this crowdfunding method.

- ✓ You will receive steady returns on your investment since it will be easier for you to predict when you will receive payments and how much you will earn due to the way the investment is structured. The potential annual return of this method is 8 to 12 percent.
- ✓ With debt investments, the risk is lower since the mortgage loan will be taken by the property owner and he is the one who has to secure it. If the owner is not able to pay off the mortgage, you will be able to recover any of your losses through foreclosure.
- ✓ This method also has a reduced holding time since debt investments are most commonly conducted with development projects. This means that the holding period will be from 6 to 24 months.

Some of the drawbacks of this method include the fact that they have higher fees when compared to the first crowdfunding method since the crowdfunding platform will probably take a particular percentage off of your payments. Also, debt investments are based on the interest rate of the mortgage loan the owner has secured. For this reason, your yields will have a cap.

Moving on, another way for you to earn passive income through real estate is to invest in such assets through the stock market. This can be done with buying into REIT or real estate investment trust. Through different ways, REITs work like mutual funds where investors purchase shares in a REIT and its managers invest the money in a portfolio that has to do with commercial properties. Generally, REITs manage or own commercial real estate properties that produce income whether this income comes from the properties themselves or from the mortgages on these properties. You will be able to invest in these companies personally with a mutual fund or through an exchange-traded fund.

Historically, real estate investment trusts have performed exceptionally well when compared to other asset classes. For example, between 1990 and 2010 the FTSE NAREIT Equity REIT Index, which is the index most investors use to calculate the state f the U.S real estate market, showed an average return of 9.9% annually and it was second only to mid-cap stocks. There are several types of REITs and if you can't decide which one is appropriate for you, you can enlist the help of a financial planner, a broker, or an investment advisor to analyze your financial goals and recommend which REIT is better based on your objectives.

One of the several types of REITs is Retail REITs. About 24% of this type of investment resides in freestanding retail and shopping malls, thus representing the biggest investment when it comes to types in America, at least. No matter which shopping mall you visit often, it is probably owned by a REIT. If you wish to start investing in retail real estate, you will have to first research well the state of the retail industry. For instance, is it a financially healthy sector now and what will be the outlook for the future?

In retail REITs, the investors make money through the rent they receive from the tenants. If the retails are in a tight spot due to poor sales and thus experience problems with their cash flow, they may delay or even default on their monthly payments. Eventually, they may even be forced to bankruptcy. If things get that messy, you will need to find a new tenant, which is not that easy, especially in this line of work. In order to mitigate this problem, you should invest in REITs with the most reliable tenants you will be able to find through your research.

Once your research on the industry itself is over, you have to focus your research on the REITs. As is the case with any other investment, it is very important that they generate healthy profits, have as little debt as possible, and strong balance sheets. Another thing you should keep in mind is that shopping has started to shift to online stores, not to the malls and this can potentially pose a problem for retail REIT space. Even though owners of the REIT spaces keep up the good job of innovation by filling the properties with tenants that are not related to retail, still the sector is under pressure.

Another type of REIT is residential REITs. Those operate as well as own multi-family rental apartment buildings and manufactured housing. Before you make an investment in this type of REIT, there are several things you will have to consider such as the fact that we tend to find the most profitable apartment markets in locations where home affordability is relatively low when compared to other parts of the country. For example, locations such as New York have a high cost of single homes and thus people are forced to rent, which enables landlords to up the price they charge per month.

.Another thing you should research in this market is the job and population growth. Typically, people move to the city because it is easier for them to get a job and the economy in cities is flourishing. Generally, a falling in vacancy rate along with higher rents is an almost sure sign that the demand in a location is rising. When the apartment supply in a location is low and the demand is rising, residential REITs should be a success story.

The next type of REIT we are going to briefly analyze is healthcare REITs. As the costs of healthcare continue to rise, this type of REIT will also flourish. The purpose of such REITs is investing in the real estate of medical centers, retirement homes, hospitals, and nursing facilities. The success of healthcare REITs is inherently linked to the healthcare system. If the funding of health services is questionable, so will be the healthcare REITs. Generally, healthcare REITs will be successful in an economy where the demand for healthcare will increase such as the rise of the aging population.

Next, we will take a look at office REITs that invest in office buildings. Basically, they receive the rental income from tenants who most probably have signed a long-term lease. If you want to invest in this type of REIT you should research the state of the economy and more specifically the unemployment rate, the rate of vacancy, the economic condition of the location where the REIT has invested, and how much capital it has for acquisitions. You should find and invest in REITs that have placed their money in locations where the economy is booming and will continue to do so for the foreseeable future such as Washington D. C.

Mortgage REITs are the next type we are going to briefly check. About 10% of the REIT investments can be found in mortgages instead of real estate properties. Some of the most famous investments are Freddie Mac and Fannie Mae which are enterprises sponsored by the government and buy mortgages through the secondary market. However, keep in mind that the fact that they are most famous does not mean they are necessarily the best. This type of investment has risks of its own despite the fact that the investment is placed in mortgages instead of equity.

For instance, if interest rates are increased it would result in a decrease of the mortgage REIT book values and thus lessen the prices of the stock. Also, if such a case happens, obtaining financing in the future will be expensive. When the interest rates are low, but they have prospects of rising, most of the mortgage REITs will trade through a discount to net asset value per share.

While you choose any of the above methods of REIT investing to earn your passive income, you should keep in mind the following:

- ✓ They should have a total-return rate of investment. They will provide high dividend yields and moderate capital appreciation in the long term. Search for companies that have been able to do both.
- ✓ Many REITs are traded most times on stock exchanges, in contrast with traditional real estate. You will get the diversification and benefits real estate investing has to offer without having to wait a long time since liquidity is important.

- ✓ Search for companies that have strong management to drive the business through difficult times. This means a management team with lots of experience.
- ✓ Invest only in REITs with reliable tenants and amazing properties.

Last, let us see how the value of REIT shares is most commonly assessed:

- ✓ Through the anticipated increased earnings per share
- ✓ Through the expected total return from a stock which is estimated from the anticipated change of price and the prevalent dividend yield.
- ✓ Through the existing dividend yields in relation to other investments that are oriented around yields.
- ✓ Through corporate structure and the quality of the management team
- ✓ Through the value of underlying assets of the real estate, other assets, and mortgages.

The last way you will be able to earn passive income through real estate investing is for you to become the partner of an active investor. Typically, investments in rental properties are an amazing way for you to build your wealth, but they can be very time-consuming. Even if you let a property manager do most of the work, you will still need to have an active role in the decisions that have to do with the maintenance of the property as well as do all the researching, analyzing, viewing, and purchasing your potential rental properties.

An alternative to the above situation is to partner with an investor that wants to play an active role throughout this process. All parties will win since it will allow you to invest your money in residential properties and let someone else, the active investor who has the extra cash, do all the work along with the managing partner. You could search online for active investors and make them an offer they can't refuse.

Generally, in passive real estate investing the main drawback is that you will get a lower return than you would if you were an active investor since the active ones will get a larger cut than you. For instance, if you are a passive partner in a real estate investment partnership, the managing partner will be paid more money than you for the time he has to put in. When you invest in a REIT, the management team that invests on your behalf will get a larger cut too.

However, this does not mean that the sacrifice of some return potential is not worth the relaxation of having someone else invest your money. This is especially true if the people, who play active roles, know how to turn your investment into a success story. Over the long run, passive real estate investing has the potential to help you build your wealth without having the usual problems a landlord or a manager of a construction project has.

High-yield Savings Account

It is a fact that high-yield savings accounts are able to offer higher interest rates than other accounts of this type and are easily accessed in the short term if you need funds. When it comes to saving and growing your money passively, you will have a number of options to choose from such as investing it, placing them into a high-yield savings account or in a checking account and it all depends on what your financial goals are. Every choice has its pros and cons.

For instance, as we have already seen when you passively invest your money, you may get better returns than with high-yield savings account, but you will not be able to access your money if they are not in liquid form, for example, if you have chosen to partner up with an active investor and decided to invest in rental properties. With a high-yield savings account, there may be restrictions when you have to withdraw your money such as penalties for withdrawing them earlier than a specif time or limits on the amount you are able to withdraw.

With investing, there is a higher risk involved, especially, in the short term. On the other hand, a checking account will allow you quick and easy access to your money, but the money you place in this type of account will typically not generate interest and if they do, it is often not much to be considered a way to generate and build your wealth in order to achieve financial freedom.

A savings account can be considered a smart decision when you want to achieve your short-term financial goals such as an emergency fund for a project you have in mind or when you want to go on a big trip. A savings account will offer you a separate account where you will be able to save money for your short-term goal and you ill not be tempted to use easily for everyday purchases as you would with your checking account. This account will also incur interest over time, so as for your deposit to grow beyond whatever you have saved.

However, the interest rates of a traditional savings account are very low. For instance, based on the information from the Federal Deposit Insurance Corporation (FDIC), in the United States, the average interest rate for such an account is 0.09%. In other words, if you made a deposit of $10.000 in a simple savings account and don't touch it for a year, you will see that after that year is over your money will be $10,009.

This may be better than no interest rate at all, but you may lose money as time passes. If you calculate the fees that were needed for your account as well as inflation, your deposit could lose its value over time with a low interest rate. The good news is that there is another option for you to achieve a higher interest rate and achieve passive income while still being able to access your money with ease. This solution is called a high-yield savings account. Let us see first what a high-yield savings account is.

This type of account is exactly what it says. It is typically a savings account that offers you a higher annual percentage yield or else APY than most traditional savings accounts. The risk involved is minimal since this stream of passive income is not an investment. Your earnings will be guaranteed by the APY proposed by the institution you collaborate with.

These accounts have minimal or no fees, at all, to open and maintain your account. The only thing you will have to do is make the deposits you wish and let your money grow as time passes. In the United States, high-yield savings accounts are also federally secured by the FDIC for $250,000 per bank, if the bank you work with is a member of the FDIC, so you should do some research before devising with which bank you wish to collaborate.

When it comes to saving for your financial needs and goal as well as generating passive income, there are a lot of options to consider. The most important thing in such situations is to research which account type benefits you the most. Let us see the returns of a traditional savings account, a high-yield savings account, a one year certificate of deposit or else CD, and a checking account if we assume that you make a deposit of $5,000 and the typical APY in the United States on July 2019:

- ✓ High-yield savings account: 2.336% - $5,116.80
- ✓ Checking account: 0.00% - $5,000.00
- ✓ One year CD: 2.55% - $5,127.50
- ✓ Traditional savings account: 0.10% - $5,005.00

From the above example, you see that a CD with a duration of one year will offer you more interest than the one of a high-yield savings account. However, one of the disadvantages of a CD is liquidity something that is seen as an advantage of a high-yield savings account. As is the case with a checking account or a traditional savings account, a high-yield savings account will offer you the chance to use your money whenever the need arises and in many cases without any penalties.

With CD, you must wait for a certain period of time until your funds mature or else when your money is scheduled to be returned to you. On the other hand, with a high-yield savings account, you are able to save up for a few months or for more than a year, time isn't the issue. If you had managed to achieve your saving or passive income goals, you will not have to wait until your money is returned to you. However, a CD may be a better choice for you if you plan:

✓ On saving and generating passive income for many years
✓ On not withdrawing your deposit for the whole duration of the contract

Instead, if you need to save up money and generate your passive income goals in a short amount of time or you need quick access to your money, a high-yield savings account will offer you more flexibility and provide you with similar profits. We do not even have to consider for your given financial goals the other two options of a checking account and a traditional savings account since their interest rate is extremely low and in the case of traditional savings accounts nonexistent. The beauty of this passive income idea is that your money are simply sitting there, growing, and waiting for you to use them.

Typically, a high-yield savings account is ideal for your short-term financial goals and for the money you want to access quickly. Let us see some goals, a high-yield savings account could help you with:

✓ Generating passive income

- ✓ Creating an emergency fund
- ✓ Saving up for college
- ✓ Purchasing a car
- ✓ Saving up money for a wedding
- ✓ Planning your vacation
- ✓ Renovating your house
- ✓ Dealing with taxes
- ✓ Preparing to make a down payment for a house you want to buy

Essentially, any plans you have for making a big purchase for the next couple of months or within a couple of years, a high-yield savings account will do the job. Also, if you are unsure about this passive income idea, you could open this type of account and keep it running for a short period of time to both check and see if you need the accumulated money to use it on something else.

If you are planning for long-term goals to generate your passive income, you could open an investment account. However, you should keep in mind that investing, typically, has more risk involved than high-yield savings account even though the market returns are considerably more than the interest rate of a savings account.

If you have reached the decision of using high-yield savings accounts for your financial goals, there are a lot of things to think of such as the fact that there are many banks as well as credit unions out there that have a plan for a high-yield savings account. Let us see the various factors you can consider to make the best choice for your saving and passive income plan.

Checking the APY is the most obvious factor, but there are other things you have to consider before choosing a high-yield savings account that will affect:

- ✓ The pace through which you will achieve your goal
- ✓ The amount through which your balance will be able to grow
- ✓ The availability of your funds

What you would want to check is if the bank you are going to collaborate with has a minimum deposit requirement. There are various high-yield savings accounts that ask for a minimum deposit in order for you to be able to open your account. If you meet this requirement, then great! If you don't, you will have to pay the same amount of attention to the minimum deposit clause as to the APY when you will select your account.

Another requirement you may come across is the minimum balance one. Some accounts will ask of you to have a minimum balance to keep in order for you to maintain the APY they offer. If you fail to keep up with this balance, you may fall to a considerably lower APY. In this case, the best option for you to be safe and secure your passive income flow is to choose another bank with no minimum balance but a lower rate. The importance of this factor is enhanced if you plan on making frequent withdrawals since you are more at risk of falling below the requested balance.

In the United States, due to the Federal Reserve's "Regulation D," you should research the transfer and withdrawal limits before you sign to open a high-yield savings account. Also, you should be aware of the fact that banks are able to impose more limits and create their own rules as well as restrictions that govern those limits and this includes the potential penalties you may have to pay for if you pass them. Those limits should be taken seriously into consideration if you plan on withdrawing funds from this account often or transfer them to your checking account.

Also, there are many banks out there who will charge you several fees to open and maintain your account. Those fees may be charged monthly, quarterly, or annually and there are many cases when these fees could cancel or even surpass the gains you will have through interest. The fees could be added into your APY by some banks while others may add the fees later, which will reduce your yield significantly

Another thing to consider is that some banks will not allow you to simply open a high-yield savings account since they may ask you first to open a checking account. The checking account may come with a minimum balance and fees of its own. As a result, even if they have the greatest APY you will find, you will have to carefully consider whether this bank is worth the extras requested.

Withdrawal options are important when it comes to choosing the bank you will open your high-yield savings account at. You will have to research the different ways you are allowed to perform a withdrawal. For example, will you be able to make online transactions or you will have to go to the bank yourself? Do they have a mobile app you can use? Do they have an ATM close to you? You will want to access your money with convenience and not have to wait to get them in time.

The same applies to your deposit options. Some credit unions and banks make it convenient for customers to make their deposits. For instance, you will want to work with a bank that will transfer your check directly to your account or set up automatic deposits. This will help you make sure that you will put funds in your account each month and not be tempted to only deposit the monthly leftovers. The easier you are able to make deposits, the more you will be motivated to go through with your financial goals.

A high-yield savings account will be the perfect choice for you to achieve your passive income goals and at the same time save some money. It is perfect for short term goals, but this does not mean you are not able to use it for your long term financial goals too since it is considered to be one of the safest options to accumulate wealth with minimum risk. Open a high-yield savings account and let your money rest and multiply while you make no effort into making them.

Investing in Certificates of Deposit

Certificates of deposit or else CDs are considered to be investments that certainly help you to grow your money in a safe manner with little or no risk involved. If you decide on using them, the process can be very simple or extremely complicated. It all depends on your needs. For instance, if you have basic needs that have to do with a steady flow of passive income, you will find it easy placing your money into a certificate of deposit and begin the process of earning more passive money than you ever did with your savings account. However, if your financial goals involve a more complex and essentially an investing strategy the process will be more complex too.

When it comes to the basics of CDs, they are considered to be a type of account offered to you by a bank or a credit union. It is very similar to a savings account from the aspect that the money you deposit will earn interest. Typically, what makes certificate deposits different from a basic savings account is the fact that they pay more interest than any other of your bank accounts. However, there is a catch to this dream. You will not be able to touch your money for a specific period of time. For instance, if you agree on a one year CD, you will not have access to your money for six months.

The time range for this type of account will vary from six months to five years. Keep in mind that the longer a CD lasts, the more they will pay due to the fact that you make a greater commitment and on the other hand, the shorter a CD lasts, the amount it will pay will be less.

However, there are exceptions to this rule with some CDs offering the option to adjust the interest rate you gain as time passes. In case you choose to withdraw your money before a CD matures, you will have to pay a penalty. Think of CDs as a type of time deposit. You make a promise to keep your money in the bank for six months and up and the bank agrees to pay you through a higher interest rate because it knows it can use your money for long-term investments such as loans. You will not be asking for your money back in a week. The time period you agree to keep your money locked up is called "term".

CDs are considered to be safe investments; therefore, they are one of the best solutions you have if you do not want any risk involved when it comes to growing your money. For instance, you may want to buy a new house in three years and you wish to save up money for the down payment through generating passive income. In such a case, you will not need to spend the money immediately as in three or four months.

So sealing your money in return for a higher interest rate is logical. If you have goals that take more than a few years, for example, retirement plans that are more than 20 years away, you should talk to a financial advisor to see if there is a better choice for this need and passive income. Keep in mind that your money is safe only if it is FDIC insured or if you are using a credit union, covered under NCUSIF insurance.

The Federal Deposit Insurance Corporation (FDIC) is an independent government agency with the task of overlooking consumer safety and banking. If your bank is insured by the Federal Deposit Insurance Corporation (FDIC), they protect you from losses if this bank closes, always assuming that your money is saved in qualifying accounts and are less than the protected dollar limit.

Even though your money is safe when closed in a bank, it still lends your money and invests it in order to earn a profit. However, if the investments do not work out, your money could be lost too. If your account is insured by the FDIC, you will be in a good place since it will replace your funds or send money to you. But the amount of money FDIC can cover has limits. You will be covered for up to $250.000 for each depositor for each bank and some types of accounts are not insured.

Due to the insurance of the FDIC, you will not have to run to the bank and save your money when the future of this bank turns bleak. Also, if you have funds that are not insured in the bank due to the fact that your deposit is more than $250.000 per individual depositor, you will be taking a risk. So, if you want to make sure that your funds are safe, research if your bank or the bank you want to collaborate with is FDIC insured. Another thing to keep in mind is that credit unions are not protected by the insurance of the FDIC. However, they get similar protection by the government under the National Credit Union Share Insurance Fund (NCUSIF).

The FDIC insurance will protect deposits at banks that are covered to the following accounts:

- ✓ Certificates of deposit (CDs)
- ✓ Checking accounts
- ✓ Money market accounts
- ✓ Savings accounts

The insurance of the FDIC will not cover:

- ✓ The money you have invested in bonds, Treasury securities, or stocks
- ✓ The contents of safety deposit boxes
- ✓ Insurance products like annuities
- ✓ The money you have invested in market mutual funds or exchange-traded funds

The items here are not insured because they are not considered as deposits even if you bought them through your bank. The insurance of the FDIC doesn't also cover theft such as identity theft, fraud, or bank robbery. However, some banks offer a banker's blanket bond that insures them from losses at ties of fire, robbery, embezzlement, or flood.

So, as far as FDIC insurance is concerned in order for you to be safe you should not have too many funds in one account or even one bank since you will be exposed to risk. Keep in mind that the limit of $250,000 is separate for every bank as long as it is under the FDIC insurance. For you to be under the FDIC coverage for more funds than the limit, you could use multiple banks or placing the money under another individual's name or spread your funds among other owners within one bank.

Returning to the topic of CDs, investing in them is quite simple since your first step is to let your bank know which one you want, for example, the six-month or the eighteen-month CD, as well as how much money you wish to deposit. We have mentioned before that some banks have minimum deposit numbers while other banks will let you put in your account as little money as you wish. When you have set up your CD, you will only have to wait until it matures and see your passive income grow. When the CD matures, you will get a notice that explains your various options. Some of them include:

- ✓ Renew the CD with another CD of the same duration
- ✓ Move your funds to a savings or checking account
- ✓ Purchase a different CD. For instance, move up for a six-month CD to a one-year CD
- ✓ Withdraw your funds

To decide which option is best for you, it would be better to review again the reasons why you are using this CD, your financial goals at the time, and reach a decision about what you should do with the money. It would be better not to let your CD renew automatically every time. You will have approximately ten days to decide what you should do. If the time passes and you do nothing, the CD will renew automatically continuing with the same terms you have agreed to before.

For example, if you had agreed to a one-year CD, asses your current situation. A lot of things can change in a year. Do you still wish to keep your money in a CD or you want to use your money somewhere else? Make conscious decisions and do not let the bank make the decisions for you. After a year or several ones, your financial goals may have changed and you'd like to make a riskier investment. If you need more time to evaluate your situation than a few days, you could move your money into a savings account and when you know what you want to do, you can invest them again in a CD.

Unless your bank is offering you something tempting to renew your original CD automatically, a pause will not damage your finances too much. Another thing you could look out for when your CD matures is what other banks have to offer after this time.

When you decided to work with your bank then, it may have had the best CD deal available, but other banks could be competitive now. Research how much passive money you can earn if you change banks and do so if the deal is really amazing. Changing banks can be a long process that takes energy and time, so your money will not generate any passive income through interest and this is the reason why changing banks should be the result of a great deal.

When it comes to CDs you could benefit from the option of "No Penalty" or liquid CDs. This is one of the various forms of CDs that banks and credit unions offer to customers and they keep creating new options to present to customers. As you have already realized throughout the course of this chapter, CDs typically have fixed rates and you would be charged with a penalty if you decided to withdraw your money earlier than the maturity term of the CD.

However, with liquid CDs, this is not the case anymore. This form of CD will allow you to withdraw your money any time you wish without having to pay an early withdrawal penalty. With this option, you will have the flexibility to withdraw and transfer your money to a CD that will pay higher if the opportunity arrives, but there is a price to pay for this flexibility.

Liquid CDs have a lower interest rate when compared to the CDs that place your money on lock up. If you look at this situation from the bank's point of view, it is logical because they are the ones that take the risk. This option would be best if you are almost certain that the rates will rise soon and you will be able to change banks or accounts in order to gain a higher rate.

Getting less passive income for this reason for a short period of time could be worth it. You should just make sure you understand the restrictions when you choose to make passive income through a liquid CD. For example, some banks impose restrictions on the time you will be able to withdraw your money and also on the amount you are able to pull out at any time.

Another form of CDs is the Bump-Up CDs which are similar to liquid CDs. After you purchase one, you will not be stuck with low interest rates if they rise in the foreseeable future. You will be able to maintain your original CD account and change to a higher interest rate when and if your bank offers them.

If this option seems appealing to you for your passive income plans, you should inform in advance your bank about wanting to exercise the bump-up CDs option. You will not get unlimited bump-up options and your bank will assume that you wish to remain with the initial interest rate if you do not inform it. As is the case with liquid CDs, bump-up CDs will pay lower interest rates when compared with the standard CDs. Again, this is a great option if rates will rise, however, if they stay the same or are about to fall, it would be better for you to choose the typical CD.

Step-up CDs will include scheduled increases in your interest rate so that you will not be restrained to rate that was in effect when you invested in your CD. Those increases may take place every six or nine months and in the case of long-term CDs, they will take effect once every year.

Another alternative you have is Brokered CDs. Those are sold for brokerage accounts and they can be bought through many banks. You can also keep them all in on account and not open one account to use the selection of a bank's CDs. Sometimes they will offer you better rates, but you should keep in mind that brokered CDs will have additional risks because instead of getting a CD directly from your credit union or bank, you get brokered CDs in a brokerage account.

As the name suggests this form of CDs is brokered. In other words, your financial advisor or yourself will assess the marketplace to discover the best CD rates. As is the case with other CDs, you will agree to lock your money up in that CD for a certain amount of time and the bank will agree to pay you a specific interest. Sometimes, you can invest in brokered CDs for a long time and they have maturity periods that are longer than the standard CDs coming straight from the bank. You could also trade brokered CDs through the secondary market, but the demand is very limited for you to attain a great price. You can also buy and sell them as is the case with other fixed-income investments. This option includes a limited supply and demand too.

However, you should watch out because this type of CD can be offered by any person who has the ability to purchase securities such as brokerage houses, financial consultants, financial advisors, or financial planners. Even you could do it through various online investing providers. One of the most important risks of brokered CDs is typically market risk and more specifically interest rate risk. For instance, you might risk selling your CD through the secondary market for less than you actually paid.

You could maintain your CD until it reaches maturity in order to avoid this risk. However, your plans may change and you wish to cash out and this is the stage where you will lose money. Brokered CDs work similarly to bonds. If the interest rates rise, secondary market buyers will not pay for face value when this investment is paying a low amount.

Another important risk you should keep in mind is fraud and scams. There have been many cases of individuals that have used brokered CDs as a way to steal money from the investors they worked with. Keep your ears open because if you hear something that is too good to be true, you are probably in danger of getting scammed. Also, brokers may not intend to scam you, but they may omit to tell you the full story of what you are getting into.

One more form of CDs is Jumbo CDs. Those, as the name suggests, have an extremely high minimum balance requirement that exceeds the amount of $100.000 in most cases. If you plan on gaining passive income through that amount of money, Jumbo CDs are the best option because you money will be safe and insured through the FDIC. Not to mention the significantly higher interest rate they will offer you.

All in all, there are several things you will need to consider if you decide to invest your money in CDs. For instance, CDs have lower risk and lower returns than other methods of investing your money and generating passive income. Your cash will be insured by the FDIC if you use a bank or covered by the NCUA insurance if you choose a credit union. Also, CDs have maturity requirements.

The CD will mature when its term is over and then, you will have to consider what you want to do next. Notify your bank for your decision before the renewal deadline or else your money will be invested in a new CD with the same terms you have agreed before.

However, it may have a higher interest rate than the initial one, but the time period you agreed at first. If the renewal deadline is not enough for you to decide, move your money to a savings account until you are ready. Another thing to keep in mind is that typically when you choose to invest in a long-term CD, the interest rate will be higher, but this option may not be the best one for your financial goals. For example, there could be high chances that you will need your money before the term is over, you will have to pay an early withdrawal penalty.

Also, there have been some rare cases of credit unions and banks that have refused to customers an early withdrawal request. If you decide to make a long-term commitment, you should also consider the state of interest rates. You will not be able to plan the time with perfection, no one can, but you could make some guesses on whether the interest rates will rise or fall. If you guess that interest rates are already high and in the foreseeable future are going to drop, a long-term commitment is perfect for you.

If you have money you don't need immediately and you wish to see growth through passive income, CDs are perfect for you. It would be good for your situation to consider a known CD strategy. If interest rates are low, there is no need for you to lock up your money in a CD that will pay you less for the next five years. What if CD and interest rates rise at some point? In this case, it would be better if you used CDs with short term commitment that will renew when the interest rates rise. The CD Ladder strategy will have you buying several CDs with each one having different terms, so they will reach maturity at different times. This will help you with having available money or money you can reinvest at dates when interest rates are up.

To better understand the ladder CD strategy, let us see an example. If you wish to make passive income out of $5,000, you can separate them in five different CDs of $1,000 each with different rates of maturity. When the one-year CD reaches maturity, you could place that money to a new three year CD, which will mature the year after another one of your CDs, matures.

You can keep this going for as long as you want until you need the cash which you will have since one CD will mature every year. With this ladder strategy, you will avoid locking all your money up and let them trapped in a low-paying CD while you will have a CD mature every year and thus avoid any early withdrawal penalties.

You can start using this passive income option with first contacting your bank or the credit union you want to work with and inform them that you want to place money into a CD. Banks will explain the different options you have and even allow you to make a CD investment online. If you don't like the online banking option, you could contact customer service or talk in person with a banker.

Explain to them how much money you wish to invest and learn everything on early withdrawal penalties and the different CD products they have to offer. When you move your money into a CD, you will see on your online dashboard or to your statements a separate account. CDs can be in nearly any account type such as individual retirement accounts, custodial accounts, and joint accounts. Just make sure to stick with NCUA-insured or FDIC-insured and do not forget to ask your banker for a better rate offer, especially if you have a heavy collaboration with them. Why not earn more passive income?

Earn Passive Income with Airbnb©

Another way for you to earn and build your passive income stream is by becoming a host on Airbnb©. Airbnb© has a one of kind approach when it comes to accommodation. As a part of the "sharing economy", it will offer to people in search of a place to stay someone else's home instead of a hotel. For instance, if a person wishes to find a place to crash while on his or her backpacking trip throughout Europe, Airbnb© gives that chance. It will also offer places for people who wish to stay in a house for even a month.

Airbnb© was founded by Brian Chesky, Nathan Blecharczyk, and Joe Gebbia in 2008. Now, recent estimates value this company of sharing homes around $35 billion. Before delving deeper into how you can make passive income as a host, let us take a brief look at how it works for guests. To start with Airbnb© does not own any properties. Instead, it works as a mediator between the people who wish to rent out their spare space and those who are searching for a place to rent.

To sign up on Airbnb© is completely free and simple. You will only have to give them your email address, your name, your birthday, and a password of your choice. You are also asked to agree to equal treatment of all people you encounter, regardless of sex, religion, and race among other factors. Once you have completed the above your account is ready and active.

Airbnb© has places you could choose to stay from all over the world considering that it has more than approximately 6 million listings through 190 countries scattered around the globe. Once you choose a listing, you can click on it and see a great amount of information about it such as pricing and check-in information, the amenities and size of that space, the rules of the house, availability, and a detailed description of that space.

You could also read reviews from others who stayed there as well as statements about the hosts. If you like this listing, you will be able to send a request to book it. Then, the site will encourage you to follow a few more steps such as giving more information about yourself. Once those steps are complete, you will be able to pay and complete your request for the space you wish to rent. After you are finished with your first booking, the process will take less time and will be much easier. However, your reservation will be final when it is approved by the host unless the space you chose is an "instant book" listing. Those listings do not have to be approved by the host.

When you wish to make passive income through this option, there are several things you will have to consider before you even list on Airbnb©. No matter what your motivation or your financial situation and goals are, you should really consider various things before you start. For instance, one of the most pressing matters to think about is your goals on listing your property or empty space on Airbnb©.

Even if you have generally thought about generating passive income through this, you have to ponder how serious you are about it. Are you looking to only make some passive money out by doing it only sometimes or you are serious about this choice and you want to make this option one of your main sources of income, if not your main one?

Depending on your answers to the previous questions, you will have to assess the amount of capital you will need as well as the risk involved.

Also, you have to keep in mind that you will have strangers living in your home. Even though it is a great source of passive income that has the potential to earn you great money, if the idea of someone you don't know to stay in your house makes you uncomfortable, then you should probably not even try it. On the other hand, if you have no problem to host and communicate with strangers appealing, you should let this option on your list of ways to earn passive income and achieve financial freedom.

A large part of your success on Airbnb© will be based on rental arbitrage. This concept is when the potential of the revenues you will gain through something are considerably more than the cost you paid to get it, you have an opportunity presented. For example, let's assume that you have a well-maintained studio apartment in LA and its expenses are $1350 per month. It is located in an extremely nice neighborhood and has ideal amenities. At some point, you learn that your neighbor is listing her studio on Airbnb© for $150 per night. With some simple calculations, you see that if you could rent your place for approximately nine days per month, you will be able to pay your rent. Now, what if you could rent your space for 27 days per month? Well, you could gain about three times the fees for leasing your place per month. A great way to make passive income right?

Some other things to keep in mind have to do with hosting considerations since hosting on Airbnb© may include more commitment and many other people involved than you initially expected. Generally, there are three types of hosts on Airbnb©. The first one wants to rent out his or her available space from the current residence only when he or she does not use the property. Usually, this happens through a carefully planned time frame during which the unit is available for rent. For example, this person may be off for a few weeks for work and wish to rent his or her residence since all the hotels are booked and knows he or she could make a few extra bucks from it.

The second of the three types of hosts on Airbnb© is the person who seeks a stable income through this chance. He or she wants to achieve a recurring and consistent stream of extra passive income from his or her property by renting it out regularly. However, still not full time. For example, those people may want to rent out the property for two months each summer or for two weekends each month. If they get the opportunity to rent their property for a premium, they will take advantage of it as well. Their aim is to maximize their profit potential, even if it takes up more of their time to do so.

The third and last type of host will rent at least one property which is dedicated solely for a short full-time rental. The ultimate goal of this host is to have a steady rental income for the one or various units he or she has and let that be the main or primary stream of income. In the end, they wish to have an entire portfolio for these short term rent plan and develop ways to automate the process as much as possible. This type of host does not aim to expand the potential profit each of the units he or she owns has, but to maximize the profit they earn each hour they have to spend on organizing the hosting business they develop.

The truth of the matter is that the more income you wish to gain through this passive income option, the more capital, planning, work, and risk you will have to take on as well as develop different strategies to make your unit high in demand. When it comes to time, you need to keep in mind that you will not simply list your property and then you will see the money come in. You will have to dedicate some time to talk with potential guests who will ask you several questions about your unit before they book with you. Your time will also be required to gain amazing reviews because bad reviews will result in a decrease in your passive income.

Initially, this may be a problem for you but as you get the gist, you will be more efficient and find out ways to save you time that are appropriate for you without lowering the quality of service you provide. To have a successful Airbnb© listing, you will have to invest some commitment and time in the process such as making certain that everything is ready for your guests to arrive.

Another thing you should consider before you start hosting is how much your unit is worth renting. For example, you wouldn't leave your job for a new one without knowing how much you will be paid. Believe it or not, there are some listings that do not have enough demand to support a hosting business. On the other hand, there are units that are high in demand and could double your salary. Research and find out which category you fall in.

For instance, you could get a market report form a data provider you trust like the LearnAirbnb© recommended AirDNA. They have detailed data for many Airbnb© markets and they will be able to provide you with a realistic assessment on how much you will be able to make through Airbnb© hosting. Do not jump into Airbnb© hosting before you make sure that your unit will have enough demand to make everything worth it.

You may also consider the need to get insurance coverage, especially if it is your own home you are renting. Most probably the plan of your home insurance does not cover damages done from short term renting. It is a fact that Airbnb© liability insurance of $1 million gives you some comfort, but if you own some special to you items or if you consider the risk of not getting covered by this policy, you will have to get additional insurance.

Also, do not forget that you have neighbors to consider when you wish to make passive income with Airbnb©. If you reside in a quiet and gated community with neighbors that go to bed early and are extremely sensitive to outsiders or people that make noise, you have to consider how they will react to such a step you are going to take. This is also true when you are residing in a unit that is a part of a community with a shared space. Even if the house is your own, you have to consider the opinion of your neighbors because an angry neighbor could seriously damage your goals of hosting with Airbnb© and earning a considerable amount of passive income.

Added to the above, you should get the okay from your landlord before you start hosting. You may not be able to host in the apartment you currently reside in if your landlord does not allow it. You could approach him kindly and explain your reasons for this decision.

However, if you have no luck with him or her, you could consider finding a new place that will allow you to host through Airbnb©.

In order to succeed in making a substantial amount of money with this passive income option, you will need to learn how to find the appropriate customers for your unit. in other words, you will need to find your target audience and as a result, you will be able to develop a profitable Airbnb© business. After you have selected your target audience, marketing will be very easy since you will know who you will have to turn your focus on and reduce vacancy rates.

People use Airbnb© for two reasons that are leisure or business and as is the case for every real estate investment Airbnb© is nearly all about location. Anyone who rents your place will do so because they wish to be close to something such as an attraction or an event. Research and discover everything that your neighborhood has to offer and this way you will have a general idea of who will choose to rent there. For example, you could answer the following questions:

- ✓ How many hotels are in the area? - If the answer is a lot, check and then compare your rates.
- ✓ Does your area have a mass or a broad appeal? - For instance, can people use it for different purposes both on weekends and on weekdays?
- ✓ Who resides in the area? - Do families, business owners or hipsters live there?
- ✓ Where is your unit located? - Is it on the main freeway or in a business district, etc.?

- ✓ What are the attractions in the area? - Do you see visitors coming for theme parks, business conferences or for its nightlife?

When you are looking for your target audience, you should also assess your property and think about which type of potential renters it can attract. For example:

- ✓ What are the amenities you will offer? - A pool, lots of space, or covered parking?
- ✓ What type is your property? - Is it a private room, a couch, or a full unit?
- ✓ What is the state of your unit? - Is your place the nicest one in your neighborhood or simply passable?

It is a fact that a certain amount of amenities will attract more people to your unit since more and more hosts bring units to the market and guests have many options to choose from. If you are serious about this option, your furniture, as well as amenities, could make all the difference in the world when it comes to hosting through Airbnb© since you will deliver to your guests an amazing experience and earn 5-star reviews. There are various ways for you to make your guest be as comfortable as possible to earn amazing ratings and some are way easier than others. The right items for your listing will be able to make the difference between a one star rating and an amazing 5 star one.

Aside from the obvious items, you will have to stock, we will present you with a list of the various other possible items that many hosts have a tendency to forget. You may wonder if you need all these things to provide your guests with an amazing experience, but the truth of the matter is that your guests may not notice that you have them, until they will certainly need them. If they find them already equipped to your unit, they will immensely appreciate the gesture and this is the attitude that wins great reviews.

The first category of essential items you must have for Airbnb© hosting is safety items. Many of the things you will see listed below are essentials that we must have in our homes too. If you see something missing for the list, you have to acquire immediately because you will be placing your guests and your Airbnb© business at risk. Let us see the safety items to acquire:

✓ Simple Carbon Monoxide Detector
✓ Nest Protect Smoke and Carbon Monoxide Alarm
✓ Simple Smoke Alarm
✓ At least one Fire Extinguisher
✓ First Aid Kit
✓ First Alert Standard Fire Extinguisher
✓ 299 Piece First Aid Kit
✓ Kidde 4LB Fire Extinguisher
✓ Non-Slip Bathtub Mat to Keep from Falls
✓ Fire Escape
✓ Non-Slip Clear Bath Mat
✓ Kidde 3 Story Fire Escape

Also, another essential service you want to include subscription and the chance for your guests to catch up on your Amazon Prime or Netflix shows. You should not restrict your guests to watch the local news on TV if their plans change and have to spend more time inside your house. Let us see the different items you can get to offer your guests easy access to such channels:

4K TVs:

- ✓ New Amazon 4K Fire TV
- ✓ New 4K Roku
- ✓ Non 4K TVs:
- ✓ New Roku Express
- ✓ New Amazon TV Stick w/ Alexa Voice Remote

If you choose to offer through your listing an effective escape from the modern world, every guest that will choose your unit to stay at will expect to have a working HDTV in your listing. There is no need for you to spend a fortune and get a fancy TV, you only want one that works, is high definition, and has access to Netflix. It is also recommended that you have one TV in the bedroom and one TV in the living room. Let us see a list of some affordable TVs for your listing that meet all the above requirements:

- ✓ Sceptre Ultra Slim 32″ inch HDTV
- ✓ 2018 TCL 40S305 40″ Roku Smart LED TV
- ✓ Toshiba 32″ Smart LED TV – with Fire TV
- ✓ TCL 32″ 1080P Smart LED TV with Roku
- ✓ Sceptre 55″ 4K LED TV icon
- ✓ TCL 55″ 4K Ultra HD Roku Smart LED TV icon
- ✓ Toshiba 55″ 4K LED TV

Another thing you should consider unless your aim is still to offer an escape from technology is the appropriate WIFI router. Your guests will most probably wish to use your WIFI, but what will be the point of you having high-speed internet if your router is not able to support it? You will need a router that can support the use of multiple devices and intense views for video content. If you need to buy a new router, you must choose one that is right for the size of your property. Let us see some routers that will work, depending on the size of your unit:

For one-bedroom and studio listings:

- ✓ TP-Link AC1200
- ✓ Tenda AC1200 Dual Band Wi-Fi Router
- ✓ For two to three-bedroom listings:
- ✓ Linksys AC1900 Dual Band
- ✓ Linksys AC1750 Dual Band
- ✓ For larger and four-bedroom listings:
- ✓ Linksys Max-Stream Tri-Band
- ✓ Linksys WRT AC3200 Smart Wireless Router

You will also have to offer your guests the ability to get some coffee even if you are not a coffee drinker. To some, good coffee can be a great way for them to start their day the right way, especially for a tired travel guest. You don't need an expensive espresso machine to achieve that. A simple coffee maker will satisfy your guests along with a french press.

There is downside to have these simple amenities to offer to your guests since those who want to drink coffee will appreciate the quality items you are offering and those who don't want one will simply not use them. You could also go a step further and offer them whole roasted coffee beans with the appropriate airtight container used for storing.

Some other items you would want to offer to your guests are digital clock and phone charging cables. Aside from the bed essentials you have to offer in order for your guests to have an amazing sleep experience, there are two other items your guests will appreciate immensely, a digital alarm clock and some extra phone charger cables. There are high chances of your guests forgetting their phone charges and this is something that happens all the time, even to people who have the best memory there is. In this case, too, you will not have to buy overpriced charging cables. You could even order them online. Last but not least, let us see a list of the most commonly forgotten items hosts forget to add to their property. Keep in mind that the items listed below are not optional. Here they are:

- ✓ An Iron
- ✓ A Dryer
- ✓ A Curler
- ✓ A Straightener
- ✓ Wi-Fi Enabled Printer

In order for you to better understand what your guests need, you could place yourself in their shoes and imagine what it would be like if you traveled in a new town or country and you have just checked-in to your Airbnb© listing. What would you like to find there for the rest of your stay?

Now let us see the process you have to go through if you want to follow this great passive income option and rent out your unit to Airbnb©. The first thing you have to do is create a free Airbnb© account. When you do that, you will see in the upper right corner the words "become a host" and click on it. After that, you have to create a listing for your unit which will seem to you a lot similar to a profile page of your space. Keep in mind that the nicer your profile is the more attention it will get, just as social media profiles. For this reason, you will have to come up with:

- ✓ A great title
- ✓ A great description
- ✓ Great photos of your unit
- ✓ A great host profile

One thing you should focus on is house rules. You should set simple and clear house rules because your guests need to know what is off-limits. However, you should not make obnoxious rules that will make no one book your unit. Also, you may have those rules on your listing, but you should also place them in the house. Most people may not even remember the rules or read again your listing before they check-in, so you have to make sure they are on the right track. Let us take a look at a few rule categories that will help you in the process of setting them:

- ✓ Extra guests: Are they allowed? How many? Do they need to be approved?
- ✓ Smocking: Is it permitted? If so, where?
- ✓ Areas that are off-limits: Are there areas, guests are not allowed? What will be the penalty for going?
- ✓ Areas to eat: Are guests allowed to eat in all areas? Is there a spot just for eating?

- ✓ Cleaning Directions: Should the guests clean the dishes? Where should the trash go?
- ✓ Laundry: Where should they put it?
- ✓ Parties or gatherings: Are they allowed? Do they need approval? What is the max size?
- ✓ Animals and other pets: Are they allowed? Are there extra charges? What size?

When you reach the part of having to price your unit, Airbnb© will help you set up your pricing by presenting you with the average prices in your area. On Airbnb©, you could also make passive income through hosting an experience. According to the Airbnb© site: "Airbnb© Experiences are activities designed and led by inspiring locals. They go beyond typical tours or classes by immersing guests in a host's unique world." If you wish to do that, review the quality standards of Airbnb© that present you with all the requirements for experiences.

The charges Airbnb© has are considered hefty, but probably cheaper when compared to a hotel stay. Guests will have to pay in addition to the rent money, a service fee of approximately 13%. Hosts will also have to pay a service fee of about three percent, which Airbnb© gets after every transaction. If you choose to be a host who offers experiences, you will have to pay a 20% service fee. Guests and hosts will not trade money up close. Guests will complete payments on the Airbnb© site when the reservation is done and they even have the option to split costs with others. Then, the host will receive the payment from Airbnb©.

This is another amazing option for your passive income plans to achieve financial freedom. It is also a choice that can help you build your own business and if you want to take things a bit further, it could "train" you for rental real estate investing if you take this option seriously and plan your steps well.

Index Funds Investing

Throughout the investing world, index funds have transformed into a major force. According to many billionaires, index funds present the most appropriate way to invest in stocks. As David Swenson said: "When you look at the results on an after-fee, after-tax basis, over reasonably long periods of time, there's almost no chance that you end up beating the index fund." Also based on Warren Buffet's words: "Both large and small investors should stick with low-cost index funds." But what are index funds?

An index fund is considered to be a form of a mutual fund, which in turn is a collection of investments such as real estate, bonds, stocks, etc., that you are able to buy. It is a package deal. Also, an index fund is able to track an index, which represents a part of a market, for example, the bond market, the stock market, the real estate market, etc.

A famous index, perhaps the most famous one, is the Dow Jones Industrial Average, which is a list of thirty blue-chip stocks. This list was created to represent a number of stocks that are of importance for the economy of the United States. The S&P 500 is perhaps one of the most discussed index around the world. It is short for the Standard and Poor's 500. This index is more complex in it methodology than the one of Dow Jones.

To put it simply, an index fund is essentially a mutual fund that does not use a portfolio manager to make the selections. Instead, this job is done by an individual committee that determines the methodology of the index. This is the case if you purchase a Dow Jones Industrial Average index fund or ETF, which is a mutual fund that is traded like a share of stock through the day and it is not settled when the day ends as it happens with common mutual funds. This is the reason why an index fund is considered to be a passive source of income because you are handing the job of the management of your money to a group that create an index and more specifically to the editors of The Wall Street Journal.

If you decide to purchase an S&P 500 index fund, which has in its collection the 500 largest companies in the United States, your money will be managed by a group of individuals at Standard and Poor's. However, you will still own your portfolio of individual stocks. Index funds have many advantages, especially for beginner investors who don't have much money to set off their career immediately and for those who wish to have an amazing source of passive income. Let us briefly see some of those advantages:

- ✓ They have the lowest costs
- ✓ They have maximum returns
- ✓ They require no effort
- ✓ They have minimum taxes

Sounds too good to be true? It is indeed true. The fund managers will invest in securities as they are in the market. It is a fact that index funds are passive since the managers of the fund do not buy and sell stocks in order to beat the market. They have as a goal to be the market. Given the nature of an index fund that has many investments included, if some stocks in the index do not perform well, your portfolio will be protected by the others. The reality is that by buying one index fund, you will be able to invest in the biggest companies in the United States.

Index funds require little cost because you will not have to pay for admin costs and the fee for your portfolio management. For example, a small investor who wants to buy shares of the 500 biggest companies in the United States and thus will have to buy 500 stocks, he or she will have to spend an extremely large amount of dollars for commissions and invest millions to achieve this. This is solved with index funds. Once you find the right index fund for your risk tolerance and needs, you will not have to spend your time on decisions and tasks that most investors have to deal with daily.

The most common categories you can buy index funds are:

- ✓ United States Stocks
- ✓ United States Bonds
- ✓ Real Estate Investment Trusts
- ✓ International Bonds and Stocks

Bonds are the way of the corporations or the government to say "I owe you". Most bonds are low at risk and for this reason, they have low returns. However, this is what places your portfolio at less risk. Real estate investment trusts are the index funds for the real estate market.

Money from investors is gathered and later used to invest in real estate properties that produce income such as international or domestic industries, commercial properties, and housing. International bonds and stocks will be perfect if you wish to diversify your portfolio. However, international stocks do not relate, typically, with how United States stocks perform. If you invest in both international and United States stocks you will be able to smooth things down.

There are some things you should keep in mind if you decide to invest in Index Funds as a way to achieve your passive income goals such as costs. Typically, index funds are considered to be low-cost investments, under 0.20%. However, you may come across some expensive ones that will cost you around 1.5%. In such a case, you should not even consider buying one that has that many costs. You should obviously invest in an index fund that costs 0.20%.

Another thing to consider the tracking capabilities since it is the job of an index fund portfolio to imitate accurately an index. To make sure the necessary accuracy is provided, you could compare the returns and holdings of the index to your fund, especially if you are investing in a small broker. Also, please, do not check you investments each day that passes.

You have used this as a source of passive income and you are better off watching a movie. No one has benefited from checking his or her investments every day. You should do that once every two or three months since index funds are the lowest risk way to invest in stocks. Take advantage of this opportunity and do not stress out over it. Last but not least, consistency is important in this case and you should set an automatic investment for every month into your index fund. This way you will be able to make more returns when it comes to your passive income. You will be given the chance to make money from the comfort of your own home without the many costs associated with other forms of investment. This is why index funds are considered one of the most effective ways a person could earn effectively passive income.

Epilogue

As you have seen throughout the course of this book, earning passive income is not as difficult as many people think and there are various ways available to make this happen and lead you to your goal of being independent and use your times as you wish. The truth of the matter is that no form and source of income is free of risk and does not require a certain amount of effort and time. Passive income is able to provide you with money you have not spend an entire day to make and have someone else take advantage of all your hard work. You will be able to see the benefits of any effort you have placed into creating a passive income stream.

When you are able to create and earn passive income, you can earn it at any given time during the day or night and from any place around the world. You will not have to be stuck on a specific schedule or job in order to make money. Once you have successfully developed one or even many different passive income streams, you will be able to see the money flowing into your account. Imagine the feeling you will get once that happens! this is the true meaning of financial freedom and you will be more close this goal than you even realize.

Whenever passive income is concerned, you will have no limit to it. There is nothing that prevents you from creating as many passive income streams as you want. The time you dedicate for such streams to be created is entirely up to you. Also, the way you want to create your passive income is entirely up to you too.

There is no limit not only to the hours you will place but to the ideas you will follow too. Passive income can be achieved through many different sources. Choose the options that make more sense for you and are based on the things you like doing the most.

You don't have to follow the schedules and ideas you dislike and do not inspire you or motivate you to achieve financial freedom. You will be able to become your own boss. Through making money from your passive income streams, you will not have to answer to anyone else other than yourself. No one will be able to question your decisions or the way you work because you will have no boss. Everything will go through you and the responsibility for the successes as well as failures will be yours.

However, you should keep in mind that creating the various passive income streams you wish will take effort and time to complete. Many people think that streams of passive income are easy to set up and need little work to start making money. This belief is a very simplistic view and can mislead many into thinking they can make money overnight. You will be required to contribute a considerable amount of your time and you may have to invest some money into your ideas too. By dedicating your time and in some cases your money, you will make sure that your passive income sources will be flowing effectively.

Even if you put all the effort you are able to, you should now that it may take a while before the passive income of your choice start to make money and becomes a stream. You need to be prepared from the beginning that it may be a while before you succeed in making this your main source of income and be able to quit your job and achieve your goal of financial freedom. In order for you to e able to quit your job and make this your main source of income, you have to diversify your tries and be certain that money will come in your account at all times.

This is a true fact because only one source of passive income will not be enough to be financially secure and free. The risk involved in having only one stream of passive income is that it can eventually dry up and leave you with no job and no income at all. So, in the case of creating many sources of passive income, you will rest assured that even if one dries up, you will have the others to cover the losses until you manage to develop it again.

Another thing you should keep in mind when you decide to create and earn passive income is that it can isolate you. This is true in most cases due to the nature of passive income. When you gave a 9-5 job, you will be able to meet new people and socialize, no matter how much you hate your boss or your job in general. You went out and met new people. While it may be a dream come true to be able to work from home and get your various chores or tasks completed through the comfort of your living room, you will have to spend a lot of your time at home, especially at the initial stage of creating your various passive income streams. For some people, who can't stand not seeing people for long periods of time, this situation may drive them crazy. If this is the case, then creating a stream of passive income, is not recommended for you.

Before you make the decision to go down this road there are several things to consider since you will have to take a step back, relax, and think about your goals. You have to be completely honest with yourself on the various things you expect to gain through this method. For instance, o you only wish to add a couple of hundred dollars to your existing income or do you wish to reach a place where you will be able to quit your job and achieve financial freedom. How long to do you plan on building your passive income streams and be able to quit your job? Where do you see yourself ten years from now?

Do you want to build multiple passive income streams because it sounds like obtaining easy money and you expect them to simply fall into your lap or those streams sound like the perfect fit for the goals you have set in your life and your general lifestyle? If you are serious about earning passive income to achieve your financial goals, the first thing you should expect is for you o have in the beginning a learning curve and a strong battle to achieve self-discipline. You will find many distractions through the internet as well as lots of sources of information. However, you should stick to your plan and choose only the sources that are completely relevant to your ideas of passive income streams.

In order to be successful in creating your passive income streams and attain financial freedom you will certainly need the following:

- ✓ A mentor
- ✓ A clear vison based on research
- ✓ A business plan
- ✓ A market
- ✓ A general plan
- ✓ A separate bank account for your passive income streams
- ✓ Determination

- ✓ Commitment
- ✓ Integrity
- ✓ Patience
- ✓ Self-discipline

In any new start you decide to make throughout your life you will need a solid plan and a lot of work to make this new start a success. Stay motivated by thinking the end result of developing and maintaining various passive income streams. Financial freedom is the end goal and you should do everything you can to acquire it. Passive income streams will offer you your dreams.

Bibliography

1. Adam Ovechkin: Passive Income: 40 Ideas to Successfully Launch Your Online Business, 4 Jun 2019.

2. Raza Imam: The Passive Income Playbook: The Simple, Proven, Step-by-Step System You Can Use to Turn Your Expertise Into Passive Income - in the Next 30 Days (Digital Marketing Mastery Book 1), 15 Mar 2019.

3. Mark Atwood: Passive Income: 25 Proven Business Models To Make Money Online From Home (Passive income ideas), 17 Oct 2017.

4. Richard James: Passive Income and Dividend Investing Bundle to Achieve Financial Freedom: The Ultimate Guide to Making Money Online in 2019. Live Anywhere, Escape the 9-5 and Live A Life of Freedom, 30 January 2019.

5. Chris Guillebeau: The $100 Startup: Reinvent the Way You Make a Living, Do What You Love, and Create a New Future, 27 Feb 2018.

6. Brandon R Turner: The Book on Rental Property Investing: How to Create Wealth and Passive Income Through Intelligent Buy & Hold Real Estate Investing!, 2 Dec 2015.

7. Chase Andrews: How to Make $100,000 per Year in Passive Income and Travel the World: The Passive Income Guide to Wealth and Financial Freedom - Features 14 Proven ... and How to Use Them to Make $100K Per Year, 7 Mar 2017.

8. Anthony Johnson: The Ultimate Tutorial for Generating Passive Online Income: Best Ways to Create Online Business

and to Start Earning Money Online and From Home, Paperback – 24 Dec 2018.

9. Millionaire Mob: Dividend Investing Your Way to Financial Freedom: A Guide to Live Off Dividends Forever, 5 Nov 2018.

10. Scott Fox: Click Millionaires: Work Less, Live More with an Internet Business You Love, 16 Jun 2012.

11. Michael Ezeanaka: Work From Home: 50 Ways to Make Money Online Analyzed (Passive Income with Affiliate Marketing, Blogging, Airbnb©, Freelancing, Dropshipping, Ebay, YouTube, ... Etc.) (Business & Money Series Book 3), 8 Aug 2019.

12. Darryl James: 30 Passive Income Ideas: The most trusted passive income guide to taking charge and building your residual income portfolio, 4 Sep 2017.

13. James Ovens: Passive Income Freedom: How to Build Your Financial Wealth and Create Independence! Emulate the Habits of Highly Effective People! Ideas of Business to Retire Early!, 14 Feb 2020.

14. Gundi Gabrielle: Passive Income Freedom: 23 Passive Income Blueprints: Go Step-by-Step from Complete Beginner to $5,000-10,000/mo in the next 6 Months! (Influencer Fast Track® Series), 6 Jan 2019.

15. Mark Morgan: Passive Income 2020: 3 Books in 1 - Complete Beginners Guide on How to Make Money Online by Blogging, eCommerce, Dropshipping, Affiliate Marketing and Amazon FBA, 23 Dec 2019.

www.ingramcontent.com/pod-product-compliance
Lightning Source LLC
Chambersburg PA
CBHW071500210326
41597CB00018B/2637